The Exploding Frog

AND OTHER FABLES FROM AESOP

Retold by John McFarland

Illustrated by James Marshall

LITTLE, BROWN AND COMPANY
BOSTON   TORONTO

FIRST EDITION

Library of Congress Cataloging in Publication Data

McFarland, John B.
    The exploding frog and other fables from Aesop.

    SUMMARY: Retells 39 of Aesop's fables.
    1. Fables [1. Fables] I. Aesopus. II. Marshall,
James, 1942-   III. Title.
PZ8.2.M19Ex   398.2'452   80-20841
    ISBN 0-316-55576-2
    ISBN 0-316-55577-0 (pbk.)

HOR
Published simultaneously in Canada
by Little, Brown and Company (Canada) Limited

PRINTED IN THE UNITED STATES OF AMERICA

Table of Contents

To Skye McKnight Keller

The Monkey and the Camel

As entertainment at a party for all the beasts, a monkey scampered onto the stage. He scooted up the curtain, swung down a tasseled rope, and danced and sang so wonderfully that all the beasts applauded wildly and cheered, "Bravo" and "Encore." A camel in the wings thought that by imitating the monkey, he too could be a star. "Now is my chance," he cried, and he galloped onto the stage. He tried to climb the curtain, but found it impossible to do. He then swung on the rope, but it ripped from the ceiling. Tripping over his hooves, he lurched through a dance routine, and he certainly proved that he could not sing a note. The camel heard only howls of uncontrolled laughter from the audience and cries of "Comedian!" "That's what I shall be, a great comedian!" he said to himself, as he ducked the tossed tomatoes.

3

The Lobster and Her Daughter

One brilliant sunny day, a lobster and her daughter were strolling down the beach. "Oh, Mother," said the daughter, "I'm so tired of being drab! On days like this, I wish so much that we could be more colorful. Think how lovely we'd look if we were a shade of red!" Her mother looked at her in horror, and shrieked, "Red! Scarlet! Magenta! I'll tell you how lovely you'd look red! Lovely enough to eat, that's how lovely! Because you'd just have been boiled to tasty perfection, you silly thing. Be thankful you're still a healthy green."

The Crab and Her Son

A mother crab was watching her son walk down the beach, and called to him, "No, no, no! You've got to stop walking sideways! It looks ridiculous! You must remember to walk forward in a straight line." The little crab then said, "If you show me the right way, I promise that I'll copy it." "All right, now watch closely," said the mother. But hard as she tried, she walked sideways too, just like every other crab.

The Country Mouse
and the City Mouse

One fine summer day, as a country mouse sat on his porch drinking a refreshing brew of swamp water and old mosquitoes, his cousin from the city arrived. "I've come for a relaxing stay at the plantation," the city mouse remarked. "When a guest arrives, it's time to eat," the country mouse said happily. When the special meal of raw grains, the finest crumbs of bread, and a big jug of homemade brew was served, the city mouse nibbled politely for a little bit and, finally, said, "You know, in the city, this is what rats eat. At home, I always end meals with a bit of cake. It's my favorite." The only reply that the country mouse could think of was "Once I found half of a broiled squab in the gully." "That is the saddest story I have ever heard! We're leaving for the city this instant," said the city mouse.

In the city, the country mouse was amazed by all the lights and excitement. "How do people get any rest here?" he asked. "Why would anybody want rest?" replied his city cousin, who hurried him right into the kitchen of a mansion. Just as the cousins hopped up onto the table to start to sample all the goodies, however, a huge cat charged into the kitchen. The country mouse raced into a hole in the wall, narrowly escaping being caught. "Well," said the country cousin, "this city life is too much for me." And he went home.

The Cat with the Cure

One day a cat overheard the farmer say that some of his hens were feeling a bit under the weather. Immediately, the cat rented some clothes that made him look like a doctor, hung a stethoscope around his neck, and, carrying a doctor's bag, walked up to the hen house. Because there was so much coughing inside the hen house, the cat had to bang loudly on the door. Finally, a raspy voice asked, "Who's there?"

The cat said, "I'm the new doctor, and I've come to see how you are feeling." The hen had already seen the regular doctor that morning and thought that this one sounded suspiciously like a cat. She replied, "Well, doctor, I think that as long as I have the strength to keep the door closed between us, I know for certain I'll just keep getting better and better."

A Wolf in Sheep's Clothing

A wolf who was always hungry had a bright idea: to fool the shepherd who always chased him away from the sheep, he would disguise himself as just another harmless sheep. The wolf found an old sheepskin, pulled it over himself, and stood in the field, mindlessly chewing on the grass right in the middle of the flock. When the shepherd drove the sheep into the pen at night, he never noticed the odd, woolly wolf. As soon as the shepherd left, the wolf congratulated himself on his good luck and started to choose the sheep he would eat first. The wolf's plan would have worked, except that he wasn't the only one hungry for mutton that night: the shepherd returned to the pen with his knife and, in the dark, slaughtered the biggest sheep of all — and that one was none other than the wolf himself.

The Lion and the Mouse

A mouse on the scent of some fine ripe cheese scurried up a hill. Just as he was reaching its crest, the earth moved. "Oh, no," squealed the mouse, "an earthquake!" But it wasn't an earthquake at all. The hill wasn't a hill! The hill was a lion! The lion, grumpy at being disturbed, grabbed the mouse by the tail and growled, "Did you ever hear the one about letting sleeping lions lie? And, of course, you know how fierce we lions can get with our enemies." The terrified mouse said, "I'm not your enemy. It was only a mistake. Please let me go. On my honor, I promise to repay your favor." The lion roared with laughter at this promise, but decided to let the amusing mouse go free. As he scampered away, making sure to avoid other sleeping lions, the mouse called back, "You wait, I'll show you how grateful I am."

About six months later, the same lion was walking through the jungle and was suddenly caught in a trapper's net. As he lay there wondering when the captors would arrive, along came the little mouse, once again rushing about his business. "Oh," said the mouse, seeing the lion in the trap, "this is a surprise!" "I'll say," said the lion. This time it was the mouse who grinned. "You remember our bargain? See these teeth? They're useful for biting more than cheese." The mouse quickly gnawed through the ropes of the net and set the lion free.

The Goose That Laid the Golden Egg

A farmer and his wife found an unusual egg under their new goose one morning: the egg was yellow, seemed solid, and was very heavy. In town, they were told that the egg was pure gold. "A golden egg! Where did you get this?" asked the townspeople. "Oh, you know... around," they replied, and hurried home. The next morning they rushed into the barn, yanked the goose by the neck, and found yet another golden egg. "This is extraordinary, but I'm not complaining," said the farmer. "If we buy more geese, we'd be even richer," his wife dreamed. They bought six hundred more geese, but the honking creatures did not lay even regular eggs. Yet the greed of the farmer and his wife increased. They told each other that only one golden egg daily was not enough. One night, they had a brilliant idea — if the golden eggs came from the goose, then they could cut open the goose to find the source of all the gold at once. Grabbing a knife, they ran to the barn, yanked the prize goose by the neck, and slit open its gut. Inside there were no golden eggs! Inside there were... insides! "Oh, me," said the farmer's wife. "Oh, my," said the farmer, holding the dead goose.

Sour Grapes

A fox was out walking one day, when he saw a grapevine growing along the top of an arbor. The luscious-looking grapes reminded him that there was no other snack quite so delicious as grapes fresh from the vine. He stood on his hind legs, but found that he could not reach the grapes with his mouth. He tried jumping, but still could not reach them. He then found an old pail to stand on, yet still fell short of his goal. The grapes were just too high up for him to reach, so he said to himself, "Now that I've gotten a closer look at the grapes, I can tell that they are obviously too green to eat and would be quite bitter. I'm so glad I decided not to eat a single one."

The Kid and the Wolf

A kid who went for a solitary romp in the woods was chased and cornered by a wolf. This kid knew that he was in trouble, but luckily he was a quick thinker and a fast talker. "I understand that wolves love tender meat. Did you know that the happier a goat is before it is slaughtered the more tender is its meat? I think that if I have to die, I would be happiest if I could dance a little first. Maybe you could play a snappy tune for me." The wolf thought this request sounded a little strange, but he was willing to try it. As he played his flute, the kid danced and danced. When the herdsman who had been searching for the stray kid heard the wolf's music as it carried through the forest, he ran toward it. He was glad when he saw the kid dancing, but then noticed with horror who the musician was and immediately drove the wolf away.

The wolf, as he ran, promised himself never to be a one-man band at his own feast again.

The Dog in the Manger

A dog had fallen asleep on a batch of hay that had been put in the cows' food trough. When the cows came into the stable, the dog, awakened by all the noise, was feeling mean. He barked and growled and tried to bite any cow that came near the trough. One hungry cow looked sadly at another and said, "I had never believed how selfish and nasty dogs could be, but now I do. Although he can't eat the hay himself, he's still going to make sure that we can't eat it either."

18

The Patient and the Doctor

A doctor, making his rounds in the hospital, asked one of his patients how he was feeling. The patient replied that he was better, except for sudden spells of cold sweats. "Ah, yes," said the doctor, "that is one of the more reliable signs of improvement." At a later meeting, the doctor again inquired about his health. "I'm just fine," he said, "except for occasional periods when all I can see is a gray blur and all I can hear is a loud buzzing." "Aha!" said the doctor, "this *is* good news! You'll be up and out of this hospital very soon." On the next visit, the doctor once more made his inquiry, and the patient replied, "Everything is about the same, but when I try to stand up, my legs collapse and I faint." "My, my," said the doctor, "this is the most remarkable sign yet that you're almost over this dreadful illness." Later that same day, a friend came to visit and asked how he was feeling. The patient whispered to his friend, "The doctor says everything is great, but I think if I have any more major signs of improvement, I'll be dead."

The Swollen Fox

A fox with an excellent sense of smell caught and followed the scent of food to a small cave. Trapped inside was a sheep, which the fox attacked. He ate the entire sheep by himself, then settled down to a delightful nap filled with dreams of special dinners and happy, flying foxes. When the fox was ready to leave the cave, he was surprised to find he could not fit through the cave's opening. "How could this be? Did one of my enemies sneak up during my nap and fill in the hole?" the fox wailed. When another fox heard his calls and came over to see what the problem was, the trapped fox told him what had happened and how some enemy must have changed the size of the exit. The listening fox chuckled and said, "No, my friend, I think that you have only yourself to blame. I'm sure that if you wait until you are again the size you were before you ate that entire sheep, you will slip out just as easily as you entered."

Disappointing the Vultures

One summer evening, a jackal and a zebra arrived at a small pond at the same time. They started to argue about who deserved the first sip of water, and soon they were trying to tear each other to pieces in a fight. At one point, when they were both getting very tired, they happened to look up and saw that vultures were landing on the trees that surrounded the pond. The jackal and the zebra knew from experience that the vultures had come to eat whichever one of them was killed in the fight. The zebra said, "Why should the vultures get an easy dinner, when the only problem here is who gets to drink first? Instead of killing each other over this, let's decide by drawing straws. Those vultures will just have to fly off somewhere else to have their feast."

The Wolf's Plea

A pack of wild dogs had attacked a wolf and left him for dead. But the wolf was strong and, after two days, he recovered. He was terribly hungry and thirsty, and in his sweetest voice called to a nearby sheep for help. "Oh, please, would you be so kind as to bring me some water? My thirst is unbearable. If I could only have some water, I know that I could get up and find some real food." The sheep heard the wolf's plea but did not trust him at all. The sheep walked away, saying to the wolf, "Yes, I can well imagine that if I were so kind to bring you water, you wouldn't bother to look very far away for a little bit of mutton."

The Mouse and the Bull

A bull was taking a nap in a field when a rascal mouse sneaked up on him and hit him in the ear with a stone. The bull woke up, in a fury, and charged after the mouse. But before the bull could catch him, the mouse ran into a tiny hole in the side of the barn. The bull would not give up the chase, however, and he butted the side of the barn again and again until he was exhausted. Although he was angry enough to tear down the whole barn, he had to stop for a bit. While the bull was resting, the mouse skittered out of the hole and bit the bull on the nose. The bull was even angrier now, and roared like a tornado. The mouse ran quickly back into his safe hole to watch the bull's tantrum. When the noise ended and the dust settled, a squeaky voice announced, "You have seen today that a good strategy from the brain of a tiny mouse can beat the biggest bull." And the mouse laughed so loudly that he could be heard over the noise that the bull made as he ran around in circles, bellowing in frustration.

The Horse's Mistake

When a man was going to market to sell his corn crop, he put the heavy load on his donkey and let his horse prance along without a care in the world. After a few miles, the tired donkey saw that they were approaching a steep hill and asked the horse to share the load. But the horse did not want to cart corn and refused. "At least until we get to the top of the hill?" pleaded the donkey. "Not on your life! That's the hardest part," said the horse, and he ran away from this boring conversation. But, halfway up the hill, the donkey collapsed from exhaustion and died. The man then whistled to the horse, and loaded everything, including the dead donkey, on the horse's back. The horse now had reason to be miserable, and said, "If only I had helped carry something earlier, my back wouldn't be heaped now with all this corn and the old carrier."

The Lion's Contribution

A fox and a lion had been hunting partners for quite a while. The fox would track down the animal, then the lion would attack and kill it. When the fox and the lion divided up the meat, the lion would take most of the catch. Secretly, the fox felt cheated. After brooding about this, the fox finally decided to end his partnership with the lion and hunt by himself. "For years, my cleverness has fed the lion. Now, I'll get all of the food for myself." On his first attempt at hunting alone, the fox attacked a flock of sheep, only to find that killing his prey was a lot harder than he had thought. It had always looked easy when the lion did it. This time, however, the sheep made so much noise while the fox tried to wrestle them to the ground that the shepherd came and drove the fox away.

The Vain Jackdaw

When the birds heard the news of an upcoming beauty contest, they flocked to the fountain to spruce up every last feather. In the midst of these gorgeous birds, the jackdaw realized, to his disappointment, that his dull feathers would not win any prizes. He was still glum, long after the others had winged off to the contest. But when he spotted old feathers on the ground all around him, he decided on a scheme! Picking the most fantastically colorful ones, he tied them to himself and glided to the hall where the contest was being held. What a furor his arrival caused! The judges, who were just about to hand the prize to a tiny painted bunting, immediately went into a huddle to change their votes. Quite quickly, the birds recovered from the jackdaw's astounding entrance. One after another recognized a familiar feather and bolted over to remove it. When the judges turned around to give the prize to the jackdaw, they saw only a pile of feathers and a dull, black and gray bird flying out the door.

Distinguished Ancestors

During their daily stroll around town, a fox and a monkey had a long and heated discussion about whose family was the more distinguished. Finally, they reached a cemetery in which there were a great many monuments and statues. The monkey stopped dead in his tracks, spread his arms wide, and spun around, saying, "My ancestors! All these were my ancestors! They were so famous and so well loved that the town erected these grand monuments to their memory!" The fox was flabbergasted at this performance, but then he, too, spread his arms and spun around, imitating the monkey, saying, "And the best part of such an incredible tale is that these famous people are much too sleepy now to wake up and call you a liar."

Belling the Cat

One bitter cold winter, when the fields were covered with ten-foot snowdrifts, all the mice huddled together inside a barn. Unfortunately for the mice, the farmer's cat who lived in the same barn loved to creep up behind the mice and pounce on them. After two mice had died from surprise attacks, and one mouse had a scare that turned its coat as white as the snow outside, the mice could stand it no longer and they called a meeting. "Enough of this has been enough," the mice said. "We need a solution!" They talked and talked, but finally agreed that if they put a bell around the cat's neck, the bell's tinkling would warn them when the cat was creeping up behind them. Everyone was relieved now that they had dreamed up this great idea, except for the white mouse that had narrowly escaped attack, who squeaked, "Ah, but my friends, who will dare to put the bell around the cat's neck?"

The Hound and the Hare

As a hare was bounding across a field, she spotted a dog racing toward her. As he came nearer, the hound charged with his teeth gnashing, growling as if he were ready for the kill. Then, just as the hare was saying her good-byes to life, the hound romped around her, wagging his tail and playing with her as if she were a dog. When the hound had gone through this game a couple of times, the hare stopped short, and said in exasperation, "I can't stand the suspense any longer. You have to decide whether you are going to kill me or ask me to become an honorary dog."

The Swimmer and the Wig

One summer afternoon, a man wearing a wig went for a swim in the lake. As he floated on his back, the tiniest wave broke across him and washed the toupee off his head. When the man looked around for the wig, he saw that it was now perched on the head of a frog. He laughed and said, "Wouldn't the person who originally grew that hair be amazed to see where it ended up?"

The Tortoise and the Hare

A hare tormented and teased a tortoise about what a slug he was. "I'm no slug; I'm a tortoise! I bet that I can win a race with you any day." "Oho!" said the hare, "not only slow but stupid to throw away money on a sure loser like yourself! Let's race today before you lose your money to somebody less deserving than I." As soon as the race began, the hare tore out and left the tortoise crawling far behind. In just a bit, the hare's lead was so enormous that he decided to take a nap under a shady tree. But while the hare snoozed, the tortoise plodded on until he crept over the finish line. After his nap, the hare gave a gigantic yawn, leapt up, and sped along the road. All of a sudden, he came to a dead stop. He was shocked to see the tortoise reclining under a shady tree just beyond the finish line. The tortoise, who held the gold ribbon and the laurel wreath crown, yelled to him, "Well now, my slug, I think I'm ready to accept your congratulations and my newly won money."

The Donkey's Favorite Foods

When a donkey and a mutt were out walking, the mutt saw a brown package lying by the side of the road. The mutt sniffed the package on all sides, and said, "All I can smell is paper." But the donkey was curious to see what was inside and chewed open the wrapper. It was a cookbook. "I was right. It is only paper," boasted the dog. But the donkey read some of the recipes from the book out loud. "Don't these sound delicious?" he asked the mutt. The mutt, after hearing about Hay Flambé and Oats Surprise, was getting restless, and said, "Maybe you could read a little faster and get to the section on Bones and Freshly Killed Cat." The donkey flipped through the book and found that there was not a word about bones or meat. When the mutt heard this, he said, "Let's get rid of the book, then; it's completely worthless and it's no wonder that somebody threw it away in the first place."

The Frog's Profession

After sleeping in the mud all winter, a frog woke up with the idea that he was, in fact, a physician. He said to himself, "Since I now know what I am, I will go out and let the rest of the world know it." When he stood on the edge of the pond and made his announcement, the other animals were stunned. A passing fox said, with a sneer, "Listen, I'm no doctor, but I think you should get some rest. You're so nervous, you're jumpy all the time; your cold is so bad that just hearing your hoarse voice makes *me* feel weak; and, besides, you're completely green! I thought doctors were supposed to cure diseases, not just display the danger signs."

Crying Wolf

A shepherd was thinking to himself, "Just another day out in the fields with nothing to do except to watch these sheep. I'm bored!" To have a little fun, he decided to give the villagers a good scare. At noontime, when everyone was sitting down to a quiet lunch, the shepherd stood on the hilltop and shouted, "Help, help, a wolf is attacking my sheep." The villagers dropped their forks and ran up the hill, only to find that it was not a wolf at all, but the shepherd's idea of a joke. The shepherd liked this prank so much that he played it three more times. Each time, the villagers got angrier and angrier at the shepherd's silliness. Then, one day, the shepherd woke from a nap and saw a wolf attacking his sheep one by one. He jumped up, and yelled, as before, "Help, help, a wolf is attacking my sheep!" But, at the shepherd's familiar cry, the villagers looked up from their work and said, "Ach! he's had enough laughs at our expense! Today we know ahead of time that it's just another of his jokes."

And the wolf was free to eat his fill.

The Grasshopper's Harvest

One winter day, when the sun was bright, the ants were taking advantage of the good weather to be outside busily hauling grain between colonies. As they were working, a sad-looking, and tired, grasshopper hobbled up to them, and said, "I wonder if you could give me some food. I wouldn't ask you, except that I haven't eaten in such a long time." The ants stopped their hustling about for a minute, and asked, "Didn't you gather your food last summer when it was time to do it, like everyone else?" The grasshopper replied, quite ashamed, "To tell the truth, I spent the whole summer singing, and never saved any food for the winter." "Well," said the ants, "with all that practice, maybe you could earn your food this winter singing in the fields. Ants, you see, have never given anybody rewards for being lazy."

The Caged Bird and the Bat

At night when all the other birds were fast asleep, a lone bird sang in a cage by a window. One night a bat fluttered around the cage and listened intently. After the bird finished its song, the bat asked why the bird sang only at night. The bird confided, "It's bad luck for me to sing during the day. One day, long ago, my singing attracted a hunter. He laid a trap for me, and here I am, locked up in this cage. I vowed then never to sing except at night." The bat was sad to hear this story, but said, "If you are already caught, it makes no difference when you sing. If you had thought of this plan before you were caught, then it might have helped you to stay free."

The Man and the Satyr

One winter day a man and a satyr were laughing about the silly saying that men and satyrs can't get along with one another. "Why," said the satyr, "there's no reason why we can't understand one another. You and I are positive proof that that saying is not true."

On a walk later that afternoon, the man started jumping up and down and blowing on his hands. "Why are you doing that?" asked the puzzled satyr. "I'm warming my hands," replied the man.

When they returned from their walk, they sat down to have some corn chowder, and the man at once started blowing on the chowder. "Why are you blowing on the chowder?" asked the once again puzzled satyr. "I am cooling the chowder a bit," replied the man. The satyr now lost his temper and started turning over furniture and throwing plates into the fireplace.

Startled by this display, the man asked, "What's the matter?" The angry satyr answered, "I was wrong! We'll never be friends. You must think I am really stupid to tell me such lies. First, you say your breath is hot to warm your hands, and now you want me to believe it's cold to cool the chowder."

The Lioness and the Vixen

One balmy spring day, a fox was gloating about her litter of healthy offspring, who were romping nearby. She turned to the mother lion next to her, and bragged, "How wonderful to see my six pups so happy, playing together." "Yes, that is nice," replied the lioness, as she watched her own cub closely while he tried to climb the trunk of a tree. Because the lioness's reply was not as enthusiastic as the fox wanted, the vixen was miffed, and said tartly, "Oh, and it *is* such a shame that you can never have more than one cub at a time."

Hearing this, the lioness, offended but confident, calmly replied, "But, my busy vixen, that one is a lion, not a pack of feeble foxes."

The Fox Without a Tail

When a careless fox had the bad luck to get his tail caught in a trap, he found that to escape he would have to leave his tail behind. Although the fox was very glad to be free, he became more conscious every day that he looked different from all the other foxes. At last, he called a meeting for all the foxes and slyly advised them, "You may all have noticed how happy I've been recently, how fast I run, how wily I am, and how good I look. I owe all of these improvements to getting rid of that old dusty, heavy, and ugly tail. If you want to improve yourselves too, the one sure way to do it is to cut off those horrid tails!" Many of the foxes were impressed by the eloquence of this speech and were discussing the idea when one of the most clever stood up and said, "Before I give up my tail, I have one question for you: would you have given us this same advice if you hadn't lost your own tail?"

The Crow and the Pitcher

A crow was flying over the desert and saw a water pitcher on the ground. She prayed that there would be some water in it to quench her thirst. When she landed, she knew her prayers were answered, for she saw her own reflection in some water at the pitcher's bottom. "I'll have a big drink," she thought, as she poked her beak into the mouth of the pitcher. But she was disappointed. Her beak was not long enough to reach the water and, as hard as she tried, she could not get even a drop. "Oh, if only I had a longer beak," she said. She looked around, and tried to think of a way to reach the water. First, she thought of tipping over the pitcher, but she knew that the water would only run out onto the ground and disappear. Then, she saw some pebbles, and decided on a plan. She carefully carried the pebbles over to the pitcher and dropped them in, one by one. Although this was hard work, with the sun beating down on her back, soon the pebbles pushed the water up to the brim of the pitcher and the crow could drink all the water. Refreshed, the crow flew on her way.

The Mole and Her Mother

One day a mole proudly announced to her mother, "Mother, I can see! I can really see!" The mother, who wanted further proof of this miracle, devised a little test and placed a huge bouquet of roses in front of the little mole. "Now, my child, tell me what you see." The little mole very confidently blurted out, "It's a goat, mother. It's obviously a goat."

"Ah, daughter," sighed her mother, "if you are still able to hear me, let me tell you that not only are you sightless like all the rest of us, but now you've also completely lost your sense of smell."

The Pig's Manners

An absentminded pig got lost during a walk, and the next thing he knew he was in the middle of a flock of sheep. "Now I'm really confused," said the pig; "nobody here looks at all like me." When the shepherd saw what had turned up, he pounced on the confused pig, and said, "What a nice roast you'll make!" Hearing these words, the pig was no longer confused. Instead, he was scared because now he knew exactly where he was headed. As the shepherd carried him away, the pig squirmed and kicked and made such a tremendous noise that the sheep, who had been dozing, woke up and called to the pig, "Why *are* you making such an awful racket and behaving so rudely to the shepherd? We are always so well mannered and gracious with him." The pig squealed, "Don't complain of my manners. You can be polite because he takes you home only to clip your wool; but for me, he's preparing a hot oven as a bed and a sauce for a covering."

The Exploding Frog

When an ox came to drink some water at a pond, the frogs, sitting on lily pads, saw how gigantic the ox was and were stunned. "Bigger than the trees," they said to one another after the ox left, "bigger than the sky." Later in the day, when the oldest frog finally rose from his sleep, they were still chattering about the size of the ox. The oldest frog asked sharply, "What is all this talk about the size of an ox? I myself can be bigger than any ox." "But," said the other frogs, "that ox was *really* big." "I've heard enough of this business," said the oldest frog, as he took a deep breath and expanded to twice his original size. "See how big I am, as big as an ox for sure," he gloated. "No, not quite that big," croaked the smaller frogs. "One more breath should do it then," he said, and grew twice as large again. "Oh," said the frogs, "this *is* amazing, but the ox was far larger." Then, because the frog hated to be bested at anything, he took a third breath. But, as all the other frogs stared at his even greater size, he suddenly exploded. "He was getting there all right," they said sadly, "but he would never have been as big as he wanted."

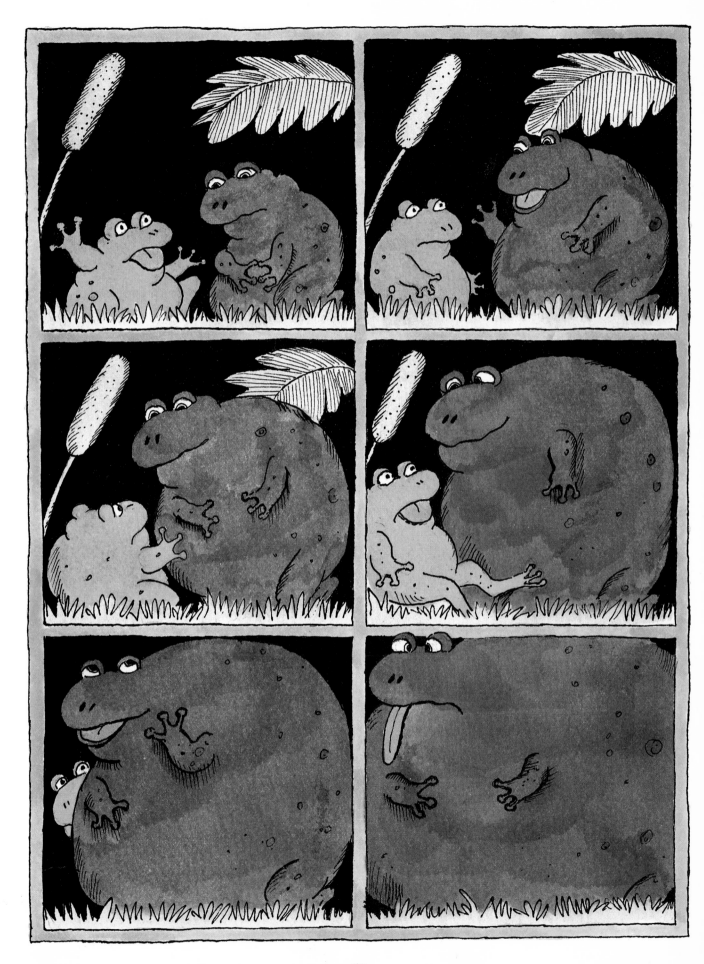